W9-BLL-352

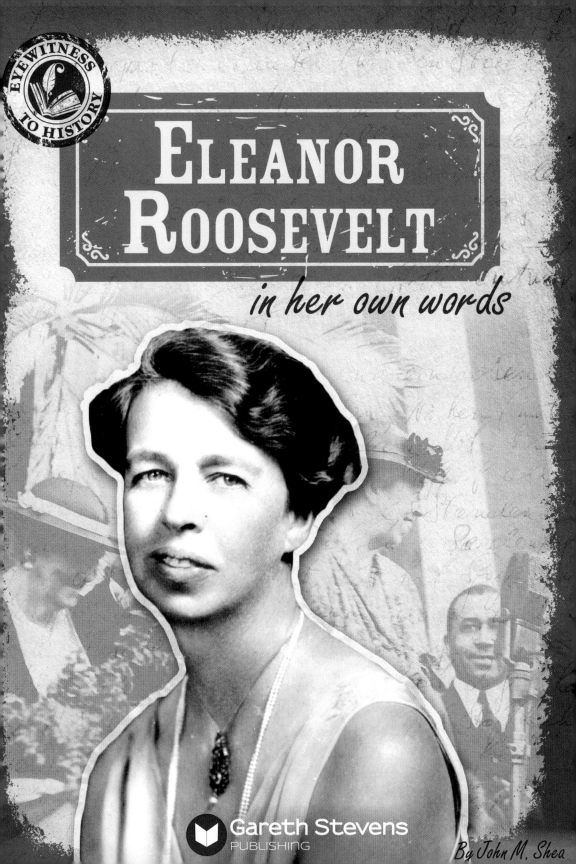

EYEWITNESS TO HISTORY

ELEANOR ROOSEVELT

in her own words

Gareth Stevens
PUBLISHING

By John M. Shea

Please visit our website, www.garethstevens.com. For a free color catalog of all our high-quality books, call toll free 1-800-542-2595 or fax 1-877-542-2596.

Library of Congress Cataloging-in-Publication Data

Shea, John M.
 Eleanor Roosevelt in her own words / John M. Shea.
    pages cm. — (Eyewitness to history)
 Includes index.
ISBN 978-1-4824-4062-1 (pbk.)
ISBN 978-1-4824-4063-8 (6 pack)
ISBN 978-1-4824-4064-5 (library binding)
1. Roosevelt, Eleanor, 1884-1962—Juvenile literature. 2. Presidents' spouses—United States—Biography—Juvenile literature. I. Title.
E807.1.R48S525 2016
 973.917092—dc23
 [B]

                                        2015028099

First Edition

Published in 2016 by
Gareth Stevens Publishing
111 East 14th Street, Suite 349
New York, NY 10003

Designer: Katelyn E. Reynolds
Editor: Therese Shea

Photo credits: Cover, p. 1 (Eleanor) Library of Congress/Getty Images; cover, p. 1 (background image) Afro American Newspapers/Gado/Getty Images; cover, p. 1 (logo quill icon) Seamartini Graphics Media/Shutterstock.com; cover, p. 1 (logo stamp) YasnaTen/Shutterstock.com; cover, p. 1 (color grunge frame) DmitryPrudnichenko/ Shutterstock.com; cover, pp. 1–32 (paper background) Nella/Shutterstock.com; cover, pp. 1–32 (decorative elements) Ozerina Anna/Shutterstock.com; pp. 1–32 (wood texture) Reinhold Leitner/Shutterstock.com; pp. 1–32 (open book background) Elena Schweitzer/ Shutterstock.com; pp. 1–32 (bookmark) Robert Adrian Hillman/Shutterstock.com; pp. 5, 7, 8–9, 11, 13, 15, 25 (both), 27 Franklin D. Roosevelt Presidential Library & Museum; p. 17 Dennis K. Johnson/Lonely Planet Images/Getty Images; pp. 19 (both), 22 courtesy of the Library of Congress; p. 21 Keystone-France/Gamma-Keystone via Getty Images; p. 23 Eliot Elisofon/The LIFE Picture Collection/Getty Images; p. 24 (signature) McSush/ Wikipedia.org; p. 29 John Greim/LightRocket via Getty Images.

CONTENTS

*Words in the glossary appear in **bold** type the first time they are used in the text.*

A FULL *Life*

Eleanor Roosevelt was one of the most influential women of the 20th century. Born to a wealthy family, her childhood was one of self-doubt. However, she grew up to be confident and well-spoken. As First Lady of the United States, Eleanor broke many traditions and faced a lot of criticism because of that. But she never stopped doing what she believed was the right thing to do. And she never stopped trying to make the world a better place around her. At the time of her death, she was considered by many to be the most admired woman in the world.

"Life was meant to be lived," Eleanor once wrote. Few people lived so fully and touched so many other people's lives as Eleanor Roosevelt did.

4

...nor Roosevelt, the first woman delegate ...he newly formed United Nations (UN), ...addresses the UN in 1946 in England. Her influence has been felt worldwide.

HER OWN WORDS

As a child, Eleanor Roosevelt was very shy. As an adult, she was one of the most famous women in the world. This is partly because she was a **prolific** writer and speaker. She wrote over 100,000 letters, more than 8,000 newspaper columns, and 27 books. She gave over 1,000 speeches. She spoke on more than 300 radio and television programs. Many of this remarkable woman's own words are used in this book.

5

Young ELEANOR

"PEOPLE AROUND ME WHO SUFFERED"

The Roosevelt family had a strong belief in helping others. As a young girl, Eleanor often went with family members to help the poor, the homeless, and the ill. *"Very early I became conscious of the fact that there were people around me who suffered in one way or another,"* she remembered. As an adult, Eleanor herself would be recognized worldwide as a friend to the suffering.

Anna Eleanor Roosevelt was born in New York City on October 11, 1884. The Roosevelts were a wealthy and well-respected family. But Eleanor's early childhood was marked with sadness and tragedy. Her mother, the beautiful Anna Hall Roosevelt, seemed disappointed in her daughter's appearance. She called young Eleanor *"Granny"* and *"very plain."*

Eleanor's relationship with her father, Elliott, was much better. He loved his *"own darling little Nell,"* and she loved him. However, he suffered from health problems related to depression and alcohol and spent little time with his family.

6

Both her parents died at a young age. Eleanor's mother passed away in 1892, and her father died less than 2 years later. At the age of 10, Eleanor was an orphan.

"I was a solemn child without beauty," Eleanor later remembered. "I seemed like a little old woman."

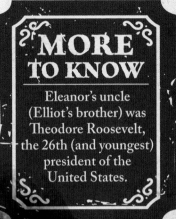

MORE TO KNOW

Eleanor's uncle (Elliot's brother) was Theodore Roosevelt, the 26th (and youngest) president of the United States.

7

ALLENSWOOD
Academy

After her parents' deaths, Eleanor's grandmother, Mary Hall, took care of her. However, Eleanor felt very alone. That changed in 1899. Eleanor was sent to study at Allenswood Academy, a school for young women in London, England. Under the school's headmistress, Marie Souvestre, Eleanor learned history, language, and literature. The classes were difficult and required hard work, but the students enjoyed them. They were encouraged to ask questions and think for themselves.

MORE TO KNOW

Schools like Allenswood Academy were one of the few places a woman could get a good education at that time. Many schools in the United States didn't allow women to attend.

Eleanor and her classmates at Allenswood Academy pose for a picture. Eleanor described her time here and with Souvestre as "the happiest years of my life."

8

Eleanor spent her summers traveling with Souvestre throughout Europe. Eleanor learned to love traveling. At the same time, she became more confident in herself. She was *"totally without fear in this new phase of my life,"* she remembered. She stayed in London for 3 years before her grandmother asked her to return home to New York.

Eleanor

MARIE SOUVESTRE

Eleanor counted Marie Souvestre as one of the most important people in her life. Born in France in 1830, Souvestre ran schools for young women in both France and England, including Allenswood Academy. As a well-spoken, independent, and confident woman, Souvestre was a role model for young Eleanor. Besides being Eleanor's headmistress and teacher, she was also her friend, and the two wrote each other letters until Souvestre's death in 1905.

9

FRANKLIN D. *Roosevelt*

IMPERFECT PARTNERSHIP

The marriage of Franklin and Eleanor was one of the greatest partnerships in American history. Their marriage wasn't always a happy one, but they grew to respect and support each other.

"My husband and I had come through the years with an acceptance of each other's faults and foibles, a deep understanding, warm affection, and agreement on essential values," Eleanor later reflected. *"We depended on each other."*

When she returned to New York City, Eleanor was expected to attend dances and social events like other young wealthy women her age. Instead, she turned her attention to helping others. She joined the Junior League for the Promotion of Settlement Movements, which worked to help immigrants living in the **slums** of New York City. She taught young students at the College Settlement on Rivington Street. She became well-known among social reformers for her hard work.

Around this time, by chance, Eleanor met Franklin Delano Roosevelt, her fifth cousin. She hadn't seen him for many years. They found

10

they enjoyed each other's company and had much in common. They became engaged and were married in New York City on March 17, 1905.

MORE TO KNOW

Eleanor's *"Uncle Ted,"* US president at the time, walked her down the aisle during her wedding.

Young Eleanor and Franklin Roosevelt are pictured here, shortly after they were married.

A TASTE of Politics

TAMMANY HALL

In 1911, Franklin ran for, and won, a seat in the New York State Senate. At first, Eleanor had little interest in politics. *"It never occurred to me that I had any part to play,"* she remembered.

While Franklin was in office, he came in conflict with Tammany Hall, a political organization that controlled New York politics for over a century. Eleanor was shocked how much power and influence this group had. She was angered by their vicious verbal attacks on her husband. Franklin's battle against Tammany Hall awoke a political awareness in Eleanor. *"That year taught me many things about politics,"* she later said, *"and started me thinking along lines that were completely new."*

Formed in 1789, Tammany Hall was a Democratic political organization that influenced New York politics. It had support from many in New York because it helped immigrants and the poor. It was popular among the working class. However, it also had a lot of critics because it was known for dishonest practices.

For example, Tammany Hall associates gave gifts to people in exchange for their votes at elections. Franklin Roosevelt eventually helped weaken its hold on New York government.

12

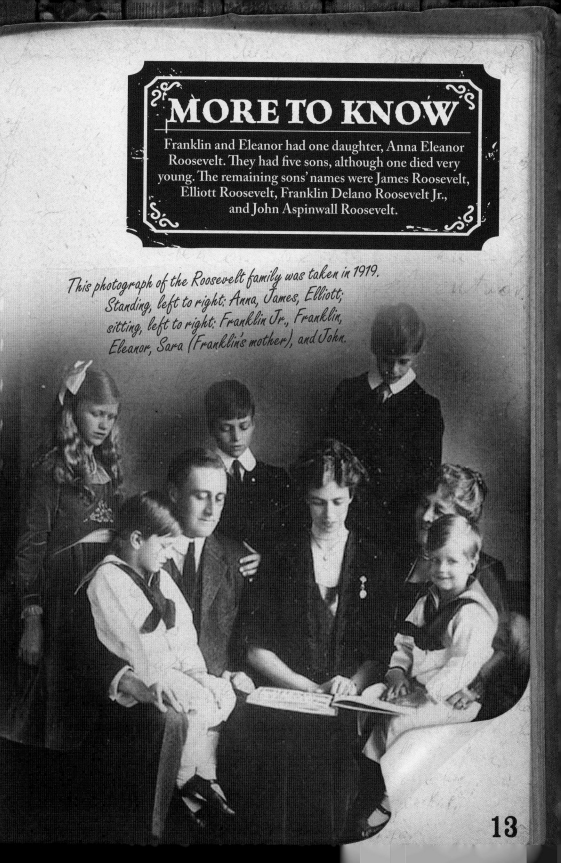

MORE TO KNOW

Franklin and Eleanor had one daughter, Anna Eleanor Roosevelt. They had five sons, although one died very young. The remaining sons' names were James Roosevelt, Elliott Roosevelt, Franklin Delano Roosevelt Jr., and John Aspinwall Roosevelt.

This photograph of the Roosevelt family was taken in 1919. Standing, left to right: Anna, James, Elliott; sitting, left to right: Franklin Jr., Franklin, Eleanor, Sara (Franklin's mother), and John.

13

WORLD *War I*

MORE TO KNOW

The term "shell shock" was first used in World War I to describe soldiers who had difficulty speaking and sleeping, intense nightmares and memories, and disorders related to their wartime experiences. Today, it's more commonly known as post-traumatic stress disorder, or PTSD.

In 1913, President Woodrow Wilson appointed Franklin the assistant secretary of the US Navy. Franklin and Eleanor moved to Washington, DC. By then, Eleanor had become *"really well schooled"* in politics.

The United States entered World War I in 1917. Eleanor joined the Navy Relief Society and the American Red Cross to help provide food and comfort for soldiers. She was asked to visit the so-called shell-shocked soldiers who were being treated at St. Elizabeth's Hospital when they returned from overseas. She was horrified to witness how soldiers with mental health problems were cared for. *"I was seeing many tragedies enacted in that hospital,"* Eleanor recalled. She pressured

14

the government to do something. As a result, Congress increased the hospital's budget, and conditions improved.

Here Eleanor is visiting a naval hospital. Her experience improving conditions at St. Elizabeth's Hospital gave her confidence to fight for those who couldn't help themselves. "I had gained some assurance about my ability to run things and the knowledge that there is joy in accomplishing a good job," she said.

THE GREAT WAR

World War I (or the Great War, as it was known then) was fought from 1914 to 1918. At first, President Woodrow Wilson promised to keep the United States out of the fight. However, German submarines sunk several unarmed ships in the Atlantic, leading to the deaths of many Americans. In April 1917, the United States declared war against Germany and its **allies**. Over 2 million Americans fought in Europe. In November 1918, Germany surrendered.

15

A WOMAN
of Influence

POLIO

In 1921, Franklin contracted **polio**. His recovery was painful. *"In many ways this was the most trying winter of my entire life,"* wrote Eleanor years later. But she admired her husband's positive attitude. *"This was torture and he bore it without the slightest complaint,"* she remembered. Polio left him **paralyzed** from the waist down. Despite his disability, Franklin became one of the most powerful individuals of the 20th century.

In 1920, Franklin ran for vice president under Democratic candidate James Cox. Cox lost to Republican Warren Harding. Franklin stepped down from politics and returned to practicing law. Free from her social duties as a politician's wife, Eleanor turned her attention to helping others. *"Ever since the war my interest had been in doing real work,"* she remembered.

As a member of The Women's City Club of New York, she used the radio to inform women about important political issues, such as child labor laws and the rights of women in the workplace. She also contributed writings to a

16

number of magazines and newspapers. She was becoming more famous than her husband had been. *The New York Times* called her a *"woman [of influence] who speaks her political mind."*

In the mid-1920s, Eleanor built a cottage in Hyde Park, New York, called Val-Kill. She considered it her home. "Val-Kill is where I used to find myself and grow. At Val-Kill I emerged as an individual," she said.

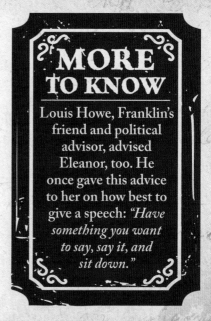

MORE TO KNOW

Louis Howe, Franklin's friend and political advisor, advised Eleanor, too. He once gave this advice to her on how best to give a speech: *"Have something you want to say, say it, and sit down."*

17

"EYES AND *Ears*"

MORE TO KNOW

Inspired by her friend and role model Marie Souvestre, Eleanor taught at the Todhunter School for young girls in New York City, even while she was First Lady of New York. *"I teach because I love it,"* she said. *"I cannot give it up."*

In 1928, Franklin returned to politics and was elected governor of New York. Shortly after, in the autumn of 1929, the United States fell into the Great Depression. Many Americans lost money in the stock market crash. Many more lost their jobs and homes.

Franklin believed that the government's duty was to help its citizens. Eleanor became an important advisor to Franklin at this time. He depended on her to be his *"eyes and ears"* at places and functions where he couldn't easily be. She inspected state-funded hospitals, orphanages, homes for the elderly, and schools. She remembered Franklin even asking her to *"look into the cooking pots on the stove"* to see if these places were making the food they claimed they were serving.

Frances Perkins

Jobless and homeless New Yorkers wait in long lines for bread during the Great Depression. Franklin's policies for creating new jobs and giving aid to those who needed it in New York would help him win the presidential election a few years later.

FRANCES PERKINS

Eleanor was influential in Franklin's decision to appoint a woman, Frances Perkins, to be New York's Industrial Commissioner, overseeing the entire state labor department. When Franklin took office as president in 1933, he appointed Perkins as US Secretary of Labor. Perkins was the first woman to serve in the presidential **cabinet**. She helped set a minimum wage, start Social Security, and outlaw child labor, among many other accomplishments.

19

A DIFFERENT First Lady

Franklin was a popular governor. In 1932, he was elected president of the United States. Almost immediately, Eleanor showed herself to be different from every First Lady before her or since. She held her own press conferences, only for female reporters, forcing newspapers to employ women. She wrote a newspaper column called "My Day" 6 days a week. She invited Americans to write to her directly. She helped bring attention to such subjects as unemployment, women's rights, and racism. Meanwhile, she continued to travel widely as Franklin's *"eyes and ears."*

Many people disapproved of her actions, but this didn't stop Eleanor. *"I'll just have to go on being myself, as much as I can,"* she said. *"I dare say I shall be criticized, whatever I do."*

MARIAN ANDERSON

In 1939, African American singer Marian Anderson was banned from performing at a concert hall in Washington, DC. The Daughters of the American Revolution, who owned the hall, said that only whites could perform there. Eleanor **resigned** from the Daughters of the American Revolution. *"To remain as a member implies approval of that action,"* she explained in her newspaper column "My Day." Eleanor later supported Anderson when she gave a concert in front of the Lincoln Memorial.

20

MORE TO KNOW

Once, while Eleanor was inspecting a prison, Franklin asked her secretary where she was. *"She's in prison, Mr. President,"* she replied. *"I'm not surprised,"* said Franklin, *"but what for?"*

Eleanor's public presence with the press was one of many things that distinguished her from other First Ladies before her.

21

WORLD *War II*

In the late 1930s, as the United States was slowly recovering from the Great Depression, another concern loomed: a second world war. Franklin was elected president for a third term on a promise to keep the United States out of foreign conflicts. But the bombing of Pearl Harbor by the Japanese

In a radio address, Eleanor admitted the Pearl Harbor attack caused anxiety and that she felt it herself: "I have a boy at sea on a destroyer. For all I know, he may be on his way to the Pacific." But she had confidence all Americans could "rise above these fears."

22

on December 7, 1941, changed everything. *"The final blow had fallen and we had been attacked,"* Eleanor said.

While Franklin was preparing his speech to ask Congress to declare war, it was Eleanor who addressed the nation first in her weekly radio program. She encouraged confidence that her fellow citizens could bear the sacrifices ahead: *"Whatever is asked of us I am sure we can accomplish it. We are the free and unconquerable people of the United States of America."*

About two-thirds of the men, women, and children in the Japanese internment camps had been born in the United States. Some died in the camps.

INTERNMENT

Two months after the bombing of Pearl Harbor, Franklin issued Executive Order 9066, which required all Japanese Americans living on the West Coast to move to **internment** camps. Many of these 120,000 people were American citizens. Eleanor opposed the internment. *"These people were not convicted of any crime,"* she wrote. While she couldn't convince her husband to reverse the order, he did allow some to leave with work permits. It wasn't until 1946, well after the war ended, that the last camp closed.

23

During the war, Eleanor traveled abroad. She witnessed firsthand the *"blocks upon blocks of rubble"* in war-torn England. She met with American soldiers in England, Australia, New Zealand, and the South Pacific. She wrote to their families about how their sons were doing.

At home, she persuaded her husband to create the Committee on Fair Employment Practices. This worked to prevent **discrimination** based on *"race, creed, color or national origin"* in hiring for jobs that were part of the defense industry and in the federal government.

In April 1945, while serving his fourth term as president, Franklin fell ill. Eleanor received a telephone call while at an event to rush to his side. *"I knew something dreadful had happened,"* she remembered. Franklin had a stroke and died before she could reach him. The United States and its allies won the war several months later.

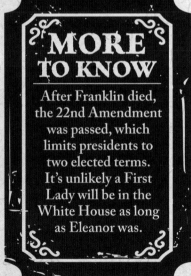

MORE TO KNOW

After Franklin died, the 22nd Amendment was passed, which limits presidents to two elected terms. It's unlikely a First Lady will be in the White House as long as Eleanor was.

Eleanor's actual signature:

Eleanor Roosevelt

24

Eleanor visits young American troops in Bora Bora in the South Pacific. "She reminded one more of some boy's mother back home than the wife of the president of the United States—and we all loved it," wrote one soldier.

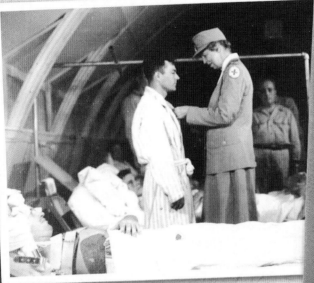

"THE DEVOTION"

Franklin died in Warm Springs, Georgia, and a train transported his body to Washington, DC, and then Hyde Park, New York, where he was to be buried. As the train traveled through cities and towns, thousands of Americans lined up to pay tribute. *"I was truly surprised by the people along the way,"* reflected Eleanor. *"I never realized the full scope of the devotion to him until after he died."*

Eleanor and several officials visit Franklin's grave at Hyde Park in August 1945.

25

HER STORY

Continues

KU KLUX KLAN

In 1958, Eleanor planned a trip to Monteagle, Tennessee, to talk about civil rights. The Ku Klux Klan, a white supremacy group, offered a $25,000 reward to anyone who killed her. Eleanor was 74 at this time. The Federal Bureau of Investigation (FBI) told her they couldn't protect her if she went. She thanked the FBI for their warning, but made the trip nonetheless. She carried a gun with her, and the Klan left her alone.

Vice President Harry Truman became the new president, and Eleanor moved out of the White House, her home for 12 years. After the death of her husband, she told reporters, *"The story is over."* However, Eleanor continued to work for change in the United States and the world over the next two decades. President Truman appointed her the first woman delegate to the newly formed United Nations. She became a voice for the **oppressed** everywhere and helped write the Universal Declaration of Human Rights.

At home, Eleanor's commitment to freedom and fairness only increased. She publically supported civil rights leaders such as Martin Luther King Jr. and Rosa Parks.

26

Regarding Eleanor, King wrote, "Her life was one of the bright **interludes** in the troubled history of mankind."

The Universal Declaration of Human Rights (shown below in Spanish) helped define the rights of people everywhere. "Where, after all, do universal rights begin? In small places, close to home," according to Eleanor. "Unless these rights have meaning there, they have little meaning anywhere."

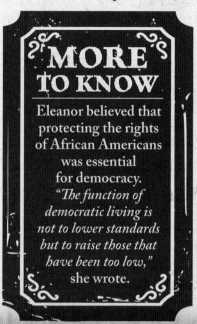

MORE TO KNOW

Eleanor believed that protecting the rights of African Americans was essential for democracy. "The function of democratic living is not to lower standards but to raise those that have been too low," she wrote.

27

DEATH and Legacy

MORE TO KNOW

Eleanor's funeral was attended by three presidents (President Kennedy and former presidents Harry Truman and Dwight Eisenhower) as well as future president Lyndon B. Johnson.

On November 7, 1962, at the age of 78, Eleanor Roosevelt died in New York City. Often criticized during her time as First Lady, Eleanor had earned the respect of nearly everyone over the years that followed. She had been voted *"the world's most admired woman"* several times in international polls. President Harry Truman called her the *"First Lady of the World."* Upon her death, Adlai Stevenson, ambassador to the United Nations, noted: *"The United States, the United Nations, the world has lost one of its great citizens . . . and a cherished friend of all mankind is gone."*

Intelligent, well-spoken, and caring, Eleanor was a remarkable woman. But perhaps most important was her determination. She never let nearly impossible tasks stop her from trying: *"You must do the thing you think you cannot do."*

28

TIMELINE
THE LIFE OF ELEANOR ROOSEVELT

1884 — Born in New York City on October 11

1899 — Attends Allenswood Academy in London

1905 — Marries Franklin Delano Roosevelt on March 17

1919 — Asks Congress to increase funding for St. Elizabeth's Hospital

1928 — Becomes First Lady of New York as Franklin becomes governor

1933 — Becomes First Lady of the United States

1935 — Starts writing her newspaper column "My Day"

1942 — Begins traveling worldwide to boost troops' spirits during World War II

1945 — Serves as US delegate to the United Nations

1948 — Helps pass the Universal Declaration of Human Rights

1961 — Becomes first chair of the President's Commission on the Status of Women

1962 — Dies in New York City on November 7

Eleanor was buried next to her husband Franklin in the rose garden of their home in Hyde Park.

FRANKLIN DELANO ROOSEVELT
1882 — 1945
ANNA ELEANOR ROOSEVELT
1884 — 1962

AN ACTIVE LIFE

Eleanor remained active right up to her death. She continued to travel worldwide, including to the Soviet Union during the **Cold War**. She remained a very influential member of the Democratic Party. She testified to Congress in support of equal pay for women. President John F. Kennedy reappointed her to the United Nations as well as selected her for the National Advisory Committee of the Peace Corps and the President's Commission on the Status of Women.

29

GLOSSARY

ally: a country that supports and helps another country in a war

cabinet: a group of senior officials appointed by the president as special advisors

Cold War: the nonviolent conflict between the United States and the Soviet Union after 1945

discrimination: the practice of unfairly treating a person or group of people differently from other people or groups of people

foible: a minor fault or flaw

interlude: a short period of time between events or activities

internment: the placement of people thought to be threats in prisons or camps without a trial

oppressed: treated in a cruel or unfair way

paralyzed: unable to move all or part of the body

polio: a disease that damages the spinal cord, making movement difficult

prolific: producing a large amount of something

resign: to give up one's office or position

slum: an area of a city where poor people live and the buildings are in bad condition

stimulating: describing something exciting or interesting

FOR MORE
Information

Books

Doak, Robin S. *Eleanor Roosevelt*. Chicago, IL: Heinemann Library, 2013

Hally, Ashleigh. *Eleanor Roosevelt*. Hamilton, GA: State Standards Publishing, 2012.

Stille, Darlene R. *Eleanor Roosevelt: First Lady and Civil Rights Activist*. Minneapolis, MN: Magic Wagon, 2013.

Websites

The Eleanor Roosevelt Papers Project
www.gwu.edu/~erpapers/
The Eleanor Roosevelt Papers Project is dedicated to preserving the writings and speeches of Eleanor Roosevelt.

The Franklin D. Roosevelt Presidential Library and Museum
www.fdrlibrary.marist.edu
The Franklin D. Roosevelt Presidential Library website is full of documents, photos, and facts about Franklin and Eleanor Roosevelt.

INDEX